Mantra Meditation: An Alternative Treatment For Anxiety and Depression

OM Channel Publications
Asheville, North Carolina

Table of Contents

Preface

After 50 years of *worse living through chemistry*, patients are clamoring for more alternative and complementary medical choices. This book is about a powerful alternative to prescription drugs for treating anxiety and depression. That alternative is Mantra Meditation.

Mantra Meditation comes to us from Ayurveda, "The Science of Life," the system of holistic medicine from India. Mantra means an "instrument of the mind," a powerful sound tool that can be used to reach a deep state of meditation -- an important tool for healing. Mantra therapy is Ayurveda's treatment of choice for both anxiety and depression. In fact, mantras are "*the most important part* of the spiritual and mental therapy of Ayurveda," according to Dr. David Frawley, leading author and Sanskrit scholar.

The book begins by tackling "The Problem with Happy Pills," a brief history of the disappointing pill-based model of psychiatry.

The Western model has let us down for three major reasons:

1. Prescription antidepressants and anti-anxiety drugs treat symptoms more than they cure disease.

2. Synthetic pills that alter brain chemistry are fraught with side effects, like sedation, weight gain, apathy and altered libido.

3. Antidepressants often work no better than sugar pills.

In Chapter 2, you will discover Ayurveda's holistic psychology, which treats the mind and spirit without the use of Western pharmaceuticals.

The real cause of today's epidemic of depression is not low levels of serotonin, or lack of any other neurotransmitter. The root cause is a lack of love and connection in life. Holistic Ayurveda uses three main tools for regaining that feeling of love and connection and returning to joy:

1. Mantra Meditation
2. Pranayama (Breath Meditation)
3. Self-Inquiry (Who am I?)

These techniques, which are common to both Yoga and Ayurveda, can be amazingly effective in calming the mind and enlightening the intellect. The ultimate goal of Ayurvedic psychology is a higher awareness, a higher consciousness, to help us understand our place in the universe beyond time and space.

As a physician who has cross-trained in Eastern and Western medicine, I can tell you that Mantra Meditation is the fastest path to this awareness, this feeling of connection with the cosmos and with each other.

In Chapter 3, meditation and mantra are explained in plain English. Of all the different types of meditation, chanting Sanskrit mantras is the easiest way to meditate. Sanskrit mantra is the core practice of Deepak Chopra's Primordial Sound Healing. It is the best way to calm the mind, especially for beginners. No experience is necessary. Side effects may include peacefulness and calm.

—

The last chapter presents the reader with seven mantras for soothing anxiety and breaking through depression, seven mantras for healing the mind and connecting with Spirit:

AUM (OM)
OM Shanti Shanti Shan-ti-hi
Asato Ma Satgamaya
Lokah Samastha
Sat Nam
The Gayatri
The Triambakam (Mahamrityunjaya)

The importance of each mantra is explained, along with its English translation and proper use. Proper pronunciation is essential for achieving the desired results, the fruit of the mantra. To experience each mantra, a YouTube playlist is provided at the end of the book.

I offer these mantras to you as a form of complementary medicine -- a sound healing alternative to prescription drugs for the treatment of mild to moderate anxiety and depression.

From the ER to the Yoga of Sound

I am often asked how I became interested in Mantra Meditation, aka Ayurvedic Sound Healing or The Yoga of Sound. I began my medical career as an Emergency Physician at a major Trauma Center in North Carolina, having completed internship and residency in Emergency Medicine in Minnesota. After 15 years of immersion in Western medicine, the constant stress was beginning to take its toll. Between the heavy patient load and the constant shift rotations, quality sleep was hard to come by. Nightmares came and went. My wife told me that my feet still moved at night as if I were running from gurney to gurney in the hospital's emergency room. She knew -- better than I -- that something needed to be done to help me handle the stress.

I did not want to go the tranquilizer or sleeping pill route and risk addiction or feeling drowsy on an early-morning shift. Looking for an alternative, she booked us both a Yoga class to see if it would help. It did. After just one hour I felt more centered, grounded and less stressed.

9

I felt increasingly peaceful at the end of each class. That was just the beginning. I was about to discover The Yoga of Sound and learn about the healing power of music and Sanskrit mantra.

One day I came home to find a present on my desk: a boxed set of three CDs, a collection of music and mantras by master sound yogi Russill Paul (Anirud Jaidev of Chennai). *The Yoga of Sound* CDs included Vedic mantras for power and protection, Tantric Mantras for creating and moving energy, and Bhakti mantras to open the heart to love. I started with the Bhakti mantras, and marveled at Russill's music.

After listening to the Yoga music, I felt better. I slept better at night. I was more calm and relaxed. I wanted to know "why" so I went to a Russill Paul workshop in California to find out. I was so deeply moved by Russill and The Yoga of Sound that I signed up for a one-year internship with the master sound yogi himself to immerse myself in sound healing. My wife and I went to India with Russill to trace Sanskrit mantra to its source. I knew I was on to something important: an Eastern method for treating the maladies of the mind -- not with pills, but with sound waves, healing sound vibrations.

Chapter 1
The Problem with Happy Pills

Do you feel anxious almost every day?

Are you sad and worried, unable to let go of thoughts that upset you?

Do you have trouble sleeping?

Have you somehow lost your joy of life?

Are you looking for an alternative to prescription tranquilizers and antidepressants?

If you answered "yes" to one or more of the above, this book was written just for you.

There is an ever-increasing body of scientific evidence confirming the power of complementary and alternative medicine like Acupuncture, Yoga, Reiki, natural herbs...and Mantra Meditation, the subject of this book. Mantras are simple chants, like *OM*, packed with energy and intention, that promote healing, insight, creativity and spiritual growth.

Before we dive deeply into meditation and mantra, I would like to address the problem with "happy pills" -- tranquilizers and antidepressants. As a physician who spent over 25 years in the ER, I have watched psychiatric drugs become more widely prescribed than almost any other medical drugs in history. According to the National Institute of Mental Health, an astounding "254 million prescriptions for antidepressants were dispensed to the American public in 2011," making them the most consumed class of medication in the USA.

The use of antidepressants has gone up 400% in the last two decades. Nearly a quarter of all women between the ages of 40-59 are taking them.
Is this a success story? It certainly is for Big Pharma, but not for the American public.

What's going on?
The answer may surprise you.

Here is the story of the "Happy Pill" and the tranquilizing of America.

The Tranquilizing of America

How did Americans become so pill-dependent and psychiatry so prescription-based? In this chapter you will find a brief history of prescription psychiatry along with some of the most serious problems associated with anti-anxiety drugs (anxiolytics) and anti-depressants.

The tranquilizing of America began in 1955 with meprobamate (Miltown) from Wallace Labs, also marketed as "Equanil" by Wyeth. These two drugs were the first to be synthesized in the laboratory and mass-marketed to society as wonder drugs for anxiety.

America responded.

Within months of their debut, the demand for Miltown and Equanil became far greater than any other drugs ever marketed in the USA. Many drugstores ran out, posting signs in their windows "out of Miltown." Look magazine and Time featured articles about the new happy pills, calling them "happiness by prescription."

Anxious?
Take a little trip to Miltown.

Stressed?
Regain your equanimity with Equanil.

A trusting and gullible 1950s public ate it up -- literally. By 1956, one out of 20 Americans were taking tranquilizers. The era of "better living through chemistry" had arrived. Even my own mother, Kitty, came home proudly showing the family her new pill bottle containing 60 Equanil tablets. She was thinking, "Now I don't have to feel anxious anymore." That's what the family doctor, the local GP, had told her. What Kitty didn't know was that taking the pills offered no cure for anxiety, just a way to cover up the symptoms. She also didn't know that the drugs were quite addictive, and had a long list of side effects starting with over-sedation (drowsiness) and apathy.

There had always been plenty of anxiety to go around: the Stock Market Crash of 1929, the Great Depression of the 1930s, followed by World War ll and the nuclear arms race of the '40s and '50s. However, people had to cope without pills. In 1955, everything changed. The era of Big Pharma had begun. The time was ripe for the tranquilizing of the USA.

In the postwar 1950s, the era of the stressed out company man and the unfulfilled housewife (for example, Madmen's Don and Betty Draper), tranquilizer pills would become as ubiquitous as Big Macs in the 1960s. The new "wonder drugs" had a dark side, however -- a side that that wasn't emphasized in the original clinical trials.

Besides mental impairment, other disturbing side effects began to appear: drug dependency, tolerance, withdrawal and seizures -- problems that would not be fully appreciated until that massive field trial of the marketplace. Many patients reported that they felt worse off than before they started the drug.

How did Big Pharma respond? An army of chemists was ordered back to the laboratory to synthesize a "new and improved" tranquilizer. Researchers were especially interested in a drug named chlordiazepoxide. In animal studies, it was noted to have a "taming effect" on a colony of aggressive monkeys. It caused a mouse to "hang limply when held by one ear." Human subjects reported feeling less tense and anxious.

The new drug, introduced by Roche Pharmaceuticals in February 1960, was given the trade name Librium, and marketed as a better treatment for anxiety -- better than Equanil.

A new class of tranquilizer, the benzodiazepine (benzo) was born. Librium soon became the number one prescription drug in the USA. The next pill frenzy was upon us.

Doctors were easy targets for marketing. They welcomed drug reps carrying boxes of doughnuts in one hand, and suitcases full of drug samples in the other. "A little bit of sugar helps the medicine go down." Just take Librium to regain your equa-Librium. Soon, however, the same old problems began to show up. Side effects like memory impairment, confusion, dizziness, loss of balance and coordination, changes in libido and even coma were reported. Adverse effects were especially apparent in the elderly. Librium dependency was found to occur in as little as four to six weeks. Many patients suffered withdrawal symptoms like panic attack, headache, insomnia, sweating, tremor, and fatigue if they tried to stop the drug.

Some patients, alarmed by the side effects, did stop taking the drug. Others went in the opposite direction. They enjoyed the tranquilizing effect of chlordiazepoxide, developed tolerance and demanded ever-higher drug dosages.

What happened next? The benzo hit parade kept on marching. With Librium under fire, Roche went back to the laboratory and, looking for a "new and improved" Librium, synthesized Valium (diazepam). The world's second benzo was born.

Valium, the "little yellow pill," was a synthetic compound even more potent than its first cousin, Librium. With Madmen-style marketing, Valium soon soared to the top of the greatest hits chart in 1969, surpassing Librium as America's most prescribed medication.

"She goes running for the shelter of a mother's little helper" sang the Rolling Stones in 1967, in the opening song of their new album, Aftermath:

Kids are different today, I hear ev'ry mother say

Mother needs something today to calm her down

And though she's not really ill, there's a little yellow pill

She goes running for the shelter of a mother's little helper

And it helps her on her way, gets her through her busy day

The song was a reflection of the sudden popularity of Valium and the ease of obtaining it from the psychiatrist or the family doctor.

Vitamin "V" became the drug of choice for anxiety, especially for those who had developed drug tolerance to Librium. A common refrain was, "Give me something stronger, Doc. My friends are on Vitamin 'V' and my Librium's just not workin' like it used to be."

Unfortunately, Valium, like its predecessor, had the same downside: tolerance, addiction, sedation, and withdrawal syndromes -- not to mention drug overdose. For many, the treatment became worse than the disease.

The last verse of "Mother's Little Helper" summed it up:

And if you take more of those
you will get an overdose

No more running for the shelter of a mother's little helper

They just helped you on your way
through your busy dying day

Prescription Psychiatry Goes Viral

Prescription psychiatry truly took off in the 1960s. For the first time, psychiatrists (and GPs), swamped with an anxiety-ridden public, could offer patients a quick fix -- an anti-anxiety pill.

Valium's huge marketing success led to a veritable flood of benzos. While some, like Ativan (lorazepam), Centrax (prazepam) and Klonopin (clonazepam), were marketed for anxiety, others, like Dalmane (flurazepam), Restoril (temazepam) and Halcion (triazolam) were marketed for insomnia.

During that time, 75% of sleeping pills were in the benzo family. Addictive benzodiazepine tranquilizers were now being aggressively marketed as sleeping pills.

The prospects for profit became incalculable. In 1986, more than 86% of prescriptions filled in retail drugstores were for benzodiazepines. Psychiatrists and family physicians wrote millions of prescriptions.

What stopped the party?

What brought "Valium-mania" to an end?

Word was getting around that, for many patients, Valium and its cousins had the same side effects as Librium. In response, the FDA finally began to restrict benzo prescriptions. Sales leveled off. Valium dropped from number 1 to number 32 on the greatest hits list. Librium became a medical footnote.

But the story wasn't over. There would be another wave of benzo-mania in the 1980s when Valium (diazepam) would experience reincarnation as Xanax (alprazolam), a new benzo introduced by Upjohn in 1981, that would become the next "mother's little helper."

Like its close relative, Valium, Xanax was effective in reducing the symptoms of anxiety, but at what cost? The risks remained the same -- sedation, addiction, tolerance and withdrawal. Even more disturbing are the recent studies which have linked benzo use with Alzheimer's dementia.

Big Pharma + Big Psych = Big Trouble

At the same time the number of tranquilizing drugs was growing exponentially in the USA, so was the number of newly defined psychiatric illnesses. Psychiatry had been busy expanding the number of mental disorders it believed to exist from 106 in 1952 to 374 mental maladies today.

How is it that the number of mental disorders has tripled since 1952?

It's about money.

The bible of "modern" psychiatry is the DSM, the Diagnostic and Statistical Manual of Mental Disorders, a handbook written by psychiatrists for psychiatrists that lists all mental disorders that psychiatrists believe to exist. It's original intent was to standardize the symptoms of each mental illness. Since 1952, however, it has mushroomed from 130 pages to 886 pages. In the new millennium, it has evolved into a promotional tool for both psychiatrists and Big Pharma.

In his book, *Cracked: The Unhappy Truth About Psychiatry*, Dr. James Davies wrote that the modern DSM "seems little more than a manual to promote the diagnosis of mental disorders to justify a pharmaceutical cure."
Are you stressed out? Can't sleep?
Take this pill.

Is your marriage unhappy? Your boss driving you crazy?
Take that pill.

Just ask your doctor.

Thanks to modern psychiatry and the DSM, normal human sadness has become "medicalized." Now anyone can qualify for a prescription. The practice of medicine has somehow evolved into the practice of marketing.

Richard Horton, editor of the medical journal Lancet, lamented in 2005 that even the medical "journals have devolved into information-laundering operations for the pharmaceutical industry." Many heads of psychiatry departments receive departmental income from drug companies.

According to Dr. Davies, "Too many leaders within the psychiatric profession have had their objectivity compromised by the pharmaceutical funds upon which they have come to depend."

The 1980s and '90s presented a once-in-a-lifetime opportunity for Big Psychiatry and Big Pharma to team up and become big bedfellows. And they did.

The Age of Prozac

What happened next became one of Big Pharma's most notable marketing successes, and years later, its most spectacular failure.

The 1980s had been the age of Xanax. The 1990s would become the age of Prozac. The attention of Time, Newsweek and the nightly news shifted. Anxiety and panic attack were yesterday's diagnoses. Depression was now the "disease of the month," replacing anxiety as the number one mental malady. As the new millennium approached, benzos were "out." A new class of drug, the serotonin booster, the SSRI (Selective Serotonin Re-uptake Inhibitor), was "in."

Its prototype was Prozac (fluoxetine).

Time magazine declared Prozac a "medical breakthrough" and the next great pill frenzy was upon us -- this time for an anti-depressant, not an anti-anxiety drug.

In the media circus that followed, Prozac's promises went way beyond depression. Researchers began suggesting that Prozac was effective not only for depression, but also for a wide range of disorders from panic attack to shyness. It was presented to the world as a panacea for coping with life's problems, even in the absence of psychiatric illness.

Fall of the House of Prozac: Low Serotonin Theory Debunked

During the 1990s, leading psychiatrists had put forth a simple theory that depression is largely a matter of brain chemistry, a deficiency of serotonin or other neurotransmitters. Therefore, an SSRI, a serotonin booster, like Prozac (fluoxetine), should be just the ticket for treatment. Unfortunately, the "leading psychiatrists" were wrong. The chemical imbalance theory was not correct. However, that did not stop it from becoming a hugely successful marketing tool. Promising everything from a problem-free personality to weight loss, Prozac zoomed to the number one drug prescribed by psychiatrists in 1990.

Despite all the promises, and despite being less addictive than the benzos, the Prozac train went off the track for three solid reasons. First came the stern "Black Box Warning" issued by the FDA in 2004: "Prozac may make some suicidal patients worse, especially young people, age 18-25." A Black Box Warning is the most severe sanction that can be given to a drug before it is pulled from the shelves.

Secondly, a consensus was developing that depression is not simply a matter of low serotonin or any other "chemical imbalance" in the brain. Attractive as that theory may sound, the truthful answer is "It's just not that simple."

Thirdly, there were accusations that Prozac worked no better than sugar pills. Professor Irving Kirsch of Harvard Medical School analyzed 38 clinical trials of antidepressants and came to a startling conclusion: the new wave of antidepressants, once heralded as wonder drugs, work no better than sugar pills for the vast majority of patients: "85 to 90% of people being prescribed antidepressants are not getting any clinically meaningful benefit from the drug itself."

Dr. Kirsch continued, "What we expected to find was that people who took the antidepressant pill would do far better than those taking the placebo, the sugar pill. We couldn't have been more wrong. Perhaps in the future, 20 years from now, antidepressants will be seen as bloodletting is seen today."

Those were harsh words from a respected Harvard professor.

Dr. Walter Brown, professor of psychiatry at Brown University, concurred: "We pretty much found the same thing as Kirsch." For mild to moderately depressed patients, "antidepressants offer no advantage over placebos, alternative therapies, or even moderate exercise." He concluded that "There is no question that these drugs are overhyped to the general public. The research shows that they are not as good as the psychiatric establishment and the pharmaceutical industry claim they are."

The depressing truth about happy pills is this: antidepressants often work no better than sugar pills. Yet, they still have the potential for side effects. The most common adverse effects of fluoxetine (Prozac) and venlafaxine (Effexor), as reported in Current Drug Safety, are reduced libido, sedation, impaired thinking and emotional instability.

Market the "Disease" As Well As the "Cure": PMS, PMDD and Prozac

The main stream media, whether TV or print, loves nothing more than a new diagnosis. Take PMDD (Premenstrual Dysphoric Disorder) for example, the condition previously known as PMS (Premenstrual Syndrome). In 1998, an panel of psychiatrists officially recognized PMDD as a mental disorder, a "new" disorder to be added to the DSM, a disorder that mandated a prescription cure.

The truth was that PMS had simply been renamed and given a new life, a more billable life, as PMDD or "Premenstrual Dysphoric Disorder."

Despite claims that PMDD is a "distinctive medical condition" that is "not yet fully understood," there was still little to distinguish it from most women's normal premenstrual syndromes (PMS). The diagnosis could be made from symptoms as vague as mood swings, irritability, tension, decreased interest in usual activities, difficulty concentrating, lack of energy, insomnia/ hypersomnia and breast tenderness.

What was to be the treatment of choice for this new disease? Had some new wonder drug been discovered?

No.

It was Prozac (fluoxetine), repackaged in pink, as Sarafem (fluoxetine).

—

According to Dr. Davies, "Lilly's patent protections on Prozac were running out a year after Sarafem would be released, so marketing Prozac under a new trade name would effectively extend patent protections for many more years." Patent protections for most pharmaceuticals are not lifelong. Corporations know that it is much cheaper to repackage an existing pill than to develop a new one.

In her article, "The Pimping of Prozac For PMS," Alicia Rebensdorf had this to say: "Eli Lilly goes on to claim that only 3% to 5% of women experience PMDD, but based on this vague diagnosis, almost every woman I know suffers from this mental disorder. The company changed the color of the pill from green to girly pink and turned the depression-stigmatized label Prozac into the oh-so-feminine name Sarafem. Yet Sarafem/ Prozac both require daily 20 mg doses of fluoxetine hydrochloride. You don't take Sarafem any less often. You don't take it in any smaller doses."

The name Sarafem was reportedly a clever play on words with Seraphim, the Hebrew word for "Angel." Just give me my Angel, and I will be OK.

To jump start sales, Eli Lilly fired up a $30 million ad campaign touting a "new" drug, Sarafem, for a "new" disease, PMDD. How many women were unwittingly prescribed Sarafem in a clever bait and switch, not realizing they would be taking Prozac (fluoxetine)?

Shyness Becomes S.A.D.

Once upon a time, shyness was not a billable condition. Then one day shyness became Social Anxiety Disorder, or S.A.D. Now we have both a "medical condition" that can be covered by insurance, and a new mandate for a prescription cure. The antidote this time was a newer antidepressant, Paxil.

Paxil (paroxetine) became another one of the biggest marketing successes of our era.

—

At first, it lagged behind Prozac in sales. However, approval was obtained for Paxil to be the treatment of choice for another "new" disease listed in the DSM: Social Anxiety Disorder, S.A.D.

S.A.D.? Take Paxil.

Sales exploded. With a tailwind of marketing, Paxil zoomed past Prozac, jumping from # 3 to # 1 in sales, a testament to the power of marketing and the media.

The Secret Formula

The secret formula that has worked so well for Big Pharma and Big Psychiatry is this: "Market the disease and market the cure."

In *The Loss of Sadness*, Allan Horwitz argued that "while depressive disorder certainly exists and can be a devastating condition warranting medical attention, the apparent epidemic of depression reflects the way the psychiatric profession has understood and reclassified normal human sadness. The real reason for the soaring prevalence of anxiety and depression disorders over the past 20 years is this: Psychiatry has been mislabeling normal anxiety and fear reactions as disorders -- disorders that mandate a prescription. Many of these millions of modern mental health patients are not crazy, or even seriously ill. Many are just like you and me, the 'worried well' -- average people simply trying to make their way navigating the normal ups and downs of life. Perhaps you or someone you know is one of them."

Market the disease...PMDD...and market the "cure" (Sarafem).
Market the disease...S.A.D....and market the "cure" (Paxil).

Market the disease...insomnia...and market the "cure" (Ambien, Lunesta and so on).

TV Advertising: Ask Your Doctor About...

As a physician, I used to think the Food and Drug Administration (FDA) was here to protect the American public. Sometimes it does. Sometimes it fails to do so. In 1997, instead of reining in the pharmaceutical giants, the American FDA did something incredibly irresponsible. It gave the green light for the direct marketing of psychiatric drugs via TV advertising. Sales soared, increasing 250% in the first three years.

Advertising drugs on television is something wisely banned in most other countries. Under pressure from Big Pharma, the United States became the only country (except New Zealand) where direct-to-consumer advertising of tranquilizers, antidepressants and sleeping pills is permitted.

Drug companies now spend $4 billion a year on ads to consumers, up from $700 million in the 1990s. The sheer number of drug commercials on TV is astonishing. The Nielsen Co. estimates that there's an average of 80 drug ads every hour of every day on American television. A sleepless nation is being carpet bombed with commercials for Ambien and Lunesta, Cymbalta and Pristiq. Impressionable American children now ask their parents for sleeping pills and antidepressants.

Today, the pharmaceutical industry rakes in over $20 billion each year from antidepressant medications alone, including serotonin boosters like Celexa (citalopram), Lexapro (escitalopram), Luvox (fluvoxamine), Zoloft (sertraline), Cymbalta (duloxetine), Effexor (venlafaxine) and Pristiq (Desvenlafaxine), along with tricyclic antidepressants like Elavil (amitriptyline), Anafranil (clomipramine), Norpramin (desipramine), Sinequan (doxepin), Tofranil (imipramine), Pamelor (nortriptyline) and Vivactil (protriptyline).

In 2015, Big Pharma is free to peddle pills and capsules, unfettered by ad restrictions, so patients can "know" what to demand from their doctors. Many members of the public are now convinced that they have a mental disorder because of trouble sleeping, or anxiety, or mild depression -- a disorder they are told can be "cured" with a prescription.

The Good News

If antidepressants often work no better than sugar pills, and anti-anxiety drugs are addictive and can contribute to Alzheimer's dementia, what are patients in this new millennium to do?

Fortunately, there are a number of more natural ways to calm the mind. As a physician who believes in alternative medicine, I recommend Mindful Meditation and Ayurvedic Sound Healing (healing with music and mantra) to all my patients, along with other holistic therapies like Yoga and Reiki, healing herbs and healing massage.

Please do consult a trusted health care provider to make sure physical illness has been ruled out. Next, if you do wish to stop your prescription meds, please do so gradually under the careful supervision of your prescribing physician.

Summary

In 1955 came the big shift -- from treating disease (mental illness) to treating unhappiness. Miltown, Librium, Valium and Xanax were each introduced and mass-marketed as wonder drugs for anxiety, each ultimately tarnished by side effects like sedation, addiction, tolerance and withdrawal syndromes. Later, Prozac and other antidepressants failed to live up to their "wonder drug" status, too. Serious side effects, like increased suicidal ideation, led to a Black Box Warning from the FDA.

Dr. Thomas Insel, Director of the National Institutes of Mental Health, had this to say: "The unfortunate reality is that current medications help too few people to get better and very few people to get well."

It's time to realize that the pill-based model has let us down. "Modern" psychiatry is largely prescription-based. Many people don't realize that a powerful prescription drug can be approved after a mere eight-week clinical trial, a trial that was designed and funded by a pharmaceutical company. The longer-term side effects often don't show up until the massive field trial of the marketplace, as was the case with Prozac.

Unlike other branches of medicine, psychiatry lacks objective testing in the lab to back up a diagnosis. It is largely a subjective specialty. A throat swab can diagnose strep throat. A urine test can diagnose a pregnancy. However, anxiety and depression do not show up in blood tests. The diagnosis is often based upon a subjective 5- to 45-minute consultation with a healthcare provider. Many physicians know that it is far easier and much more lucrative to write a prescription than it is to provide 45 minutes of talk therapy.

Many psychiatrists feel trapped by a system that pushes them to opt for a quick fix rather than a long-term solution. "Physicians have less and less time to spend with patients or may see them only occasionally, when their talk therapist sends them in for drugs," noted Dr. Harold J. Bursztajn, associate clinical professor of psychiatry at Harvard Medical School. "Anxiety can almost always be treated in other ways, but too many doctors are too rushed to search for the root of a patient's problem when there's a supposed solution that seems quick, easy and effective."

Fortunately, a number of psychiatrists are going holistic. They are using mindfulness meditation, mantra and natural herbs as treatments of choice and using Western medicines only as a last resort.

The truth about the human condition is this: we all have up and down cycles in our lives. It is normal to feel some level of depression before and after major life changes: the death of a loved one, illness or injury, a divorce or loss of a job. Minor depression can also be a form of "time out" for adults. It can be nature's way of giving us a rest, a time to go within and be reflective. Anxiety can be a message from the psyche telling us to re-evaluate our lives, an inner call to find our true sense of purpose in life.

Symptoms of sadness and anxiety do not always require prescription drugs. Alternative treatments, like meditation and mantra, often work just as well or better, without debilitating side effects like mental impairment, weight gain, decreased libido, or drug withdrawal. Find out how in Chapters 2 and 3 as we focus on Ayurveda's holistic psychology.

In Chapter 4, you will learn seven healing Sanskrit mantras from the Yoga of Sound tradition, seven mantras for home practice.

Chapter 2
Ayurveda's Holistic Psychology

After 50 years of worse living through chemistry, stressed out patients in this new millennium are seeking more alternative and complementary medical choices. In this chapter, you will discover how to treat the body-mind and Spirit with Ayurveda's holistic psychology, without the need for Western pharmaceuticals.

First, let's start with some key definitions:

Ayurveda The holistic medicine from India (literally, The Knowledge of Life and Longevity).

Holistic Taking all of one's needs into consideration: physical, mental, and Spiritual. A holistic philosophy even recognizes the importance of social needs like food, a good salary, adequate housing and access to health care.

—

Psychologist Someone who has earned a doctoral-level degree in psychology, and who has become licensed in providing psychological services to the public.

Note: Many Social workers (MSWs) become psychological therapists having earned a masters degree in social work. They are specifically trained in psychotherapy, working with patients by listening and talking with them. Some Advanced Psychiatric Nurses (APNs) perform this function, too.

Psychiatrist A medical doctor who is trained in treating mental illnesses and mood disorders with medications.

One of the biggest differences between psychiatrists and psychologists is that only psychiatrists can prescribe pharmaceuticals and administer ECT (Electro-Convulsive Therapy), except in New Mexico and Louisiana, where some psychologists are allowed to prescribe.

Alternative Medicine refers to a non-mainstream approach in place of conventional medicine.

—

Complementary Medicine refers to a treatment method used in addition to conventional medicine.

The Ayurvedic Approach

In India, a country with over one billion people, Ayurveda has evolved over the past 5,000 years, as did Chinese medicine farther to the East. It is the medicine of the future coming to us from the distant past. With Ayurveda, the emphasis is on the prevention of illness. This highest level of healing eliminates diseases before they happen.

When it comes to treating anxiety and depression, Ayurveda does not use the synthetic pharmaceuticals so prevalent in the West. Instead, holistic Ayurveda recommends these natural treatments:

1. Ayurvedic massage with herb-infused oils
2. Healing herbs by mouth
3. Mantra Meditation (aka Ayurvedic Sound Healing or The Yoga of Sound)
4. An Ayurvedic diet, in which healing foods become medicines

—

5. Yoga (the eight-part yoga system)
6. Ayurvedic Psychological Counseling (APC)

Ayurvedic doctors prescribe a special type of healing massage, using oils infused with medicinal herbs. When the body is relaxed, the mind naturally follows...into a deep, deep tranquility. The herbs are selected based on one's mind-body type, or dosha: Vata, Pitta or Kapha. Physically speaking, Vata frames are tall and skinny, Pittas are medium build and muscular and Kapha types are large framed and stocky. In temperament, Vata types are lively and enthusiastic by nature, and thrive on change. Pitta people are purposeful and intense, and love to convince. Kapha folks are easy going, accepting and like to support.

In Ayurvedic massage, special attention is given to the marma (acupressure) points to promote the flow of healing energy, called prana in India, or chi in the acupuncture tradition.

Natural herbs by mouth, like Ashwagandha (Indian Ginseng), are also recommended as a tonic for the nervous system. However, the most important Ayurvedic treatment for anxiety and depression is not herbal. It is sound healing with Mantra Meditation from the Ayurvedic/Yoga of Sound (YOS) tradition. The Yoga of Sound is the yoga of music and mantra.

Mantra Meditation is considered Ayurveda's most effective therapy for anxiety, depression and insomnia. Yet Mantra Therapy remains one of the least known treatments in the West.

Mantra is a Sanskrit term that means a "tool of the mind." It is a tool that when used properly, can take us into a place of tranquility and calm. Dr. Deepak Chopra calls it "the place of pure awareness...the unconditioned mind... the source of thought."

The unconditioned mind is the clean slate mind, the empty mind. It is the mind before it gets programmed with criticism and praise, successes and failures, hurts and grievances and so on.

The intention of this book is to introduce the beginner to Mantra Meditation as the simplest, easiest and most effective way to

—

calm the mind and to access that place of pure awareness, peacefulness and bliss.

* * *

In my experience, most patients with mild to moderate anxiety and depression can be successfully treated by Ayurvedic means alone...without the prescription pad. These Eastern treatment methods have helped many patients eliminate their dependency on antidepressants, tranquilizers and even opiates.

"The doctor of the future will give no medication, but will interest his patients in the care of the human frame, diet and in the cause and prevention of disease."
                                    -Thomas Edison (1903)

Understanding the Mind

The first step in healing the mind is understanding the mind. *The mind belongs to us but is not who we really are.* The human mind is made up of a ticker-tape of thoughts and counter thoughts, estimated at about

45,000 per day. We are always thinking about something -- goals, basic enjoyments, things we need, or things we want. Often filled with anxious thoughts and fears, the monkey mind is constantly calculating or repeating, calculating or repeating.

Are your thoughts filled with critical self-talk, with conflict and unhappiness? Do you daily relive some previous tragedy or disappointment that became deeply etched into your mind?

Or...

Are your thoughts peaceful and harmonious, filled with love and gratitude, and characterized by a fascination for life?

A Native American elder once told his grandson, "I have two wolves fighting in my heart. One wolf is full of anger, resentment, jealousy, hatred and fear. The other is full of love, compassion, joy, generosity and truth." When asked which wolf will win the fight, the wise elder replied, "The one I feed."

The quality of your life is determined by how you think, by where you put your energy and awareness. Energy follows thought. Every action begins with a thought.

The Mind and the Car's Computer

The holistic body-mind-Spirit has been compared to the car. The physical body is like the body of the car, prone to rust and breakdown. The mind, the ego-personality, is like the car's computer, a computer easily programmed by social pressures or the whims of the media, by likes and dislikes, loves and hates.

With its endless thoughts and counter-thoughts, the ego is the troublemaker, the one that is easily offended, or angry, or anxious, or sad.

"No one liked me on Facebook today" said the ego-personality with a frown. "Can you believe what he said about me in that Tweet?" In the noisy mind, thoughts and counter-thoughts are so prevalent that it becomes easy to believe that we *are* our thoughts.

When the mind is stilled by meditation, the higher Self, the Soul-Self, predominates. The car's true driver is not the computer. It is this Soul Self, the one we like to see behind the wheel. Think of this higher Self as your elder, the real you beyond all fear, all emotional upset, all dramas...the one who "knows."

Swami Muktananda of India put it this way:

There is a being inside you who knows everything.
Try to understand him.
He is Consciousness. He is the Self.
Because He exists, you exist.
He is the experience of "I am."

If you don't understand the higher Self, it may be because you haven't felt him/her in a while. The ego personality may be so wrapped up in anger, jealousy, hurt, grievance or envy that it doesn't realize that there is a higher Self there at all, standing like an elder waiting for a prodigal son to come home.

Who do you want to be in charge, the ego-mind, the everyday self, with all of its worries and compulsions, or the Higher Self, the Spirit, the Soul-Self, the one who can watch the mind's thoughts come and go without being tangled up by them?

We must take charge of our minds, so the computer becomes just an instrument and not the driver of the car.

What is the first step toward controlling the mind? Take charge of your thoughts by becoming the watcher of your thoughts. Watch the thoughts go by like bubbles, as if you were sitting beside a creek with a bubble blower. You blew the bubble...you created that thought. Now watch it float away.

See how many times you can "catch yourself thinking"...thinking about tomorrow or worrying about something that happened last month or last year. When you "catch yourself thinking," your journey toward Awareness has begun.

Awareness (Consciousness): The Ultimate Goal

"Awareness is nothing less than the discovery of our true nature, the realization of our place in the Universe...beyond time and space. True awareness is the ultimate cure for all psychological disorders."

Dr. David Frawley

If you realize who you really are, a Soul-Self inhabiting a physical body for a few years on Earth, there is no way you will feel anxious or depressed. You will feel joyful, with a joy that comes from within. Such awareness does not come in pill form. It is most readily achieved through meditation, starting with Mantra Meditation.

In gaining control of our minds, we stop being the victims of what goes on in our minds. We discover who we really are and what we really need. We discover our place in the Universe beyond space and time.

You are not your thoughts. You are not the mind.

—

You are a being of Light made of conscious energy, whose natural state is beauty, consciousness (awareness) and bliss. This bliss state, this state of higher consciousness, is available to you through mantra and other forms of meditation.

Next let's take a closer look at the real causes of anxiety and depression. The answers may surprise you. Then we will examine Ayurveda's alternative treatments in more detail.

Anxiety and Panic Attack

During my 25 years in the Emergency Room, I witnessed a steady increase in the number of patients suffering from anxiety and panic attack. Stress related illnesses far out-numbered the GSWs (Gun Shot Wounds) and MVCs (Motor Vehicle Collisions) in our ER. The stress would manifest in a variety of ways...high blood pressure, heart attacks, panic attacks, ulcers, stroke, overdoses, even suicides.

Panic attacks are like anxiety on steroids. They often occur out of the blue and are characterized by extreme anxiety, hyperventilation and chest tightness. The common refrain of the panic attack patient is "I feel like I'm going to die."

What is the initial treatment of panic attack in the ER -- at the triage desk?

Xanax? Valium?

No.
It is not a pill. It is a breath meditation, not a medication.

In Raleigh, N.C., our Trauma Center ER was blessed with heart-centered triage nurses. When patients would present with panic attack and hyperventilation, the nurse on the front line would say, with a reassuring hand on the shoulder, "OK, hon, you are having a panic attack. Here is what we need to do. First, slow your breathing down...breathe *with* me... in... and out. In... and out. Inhale. Exhale. Inhale. Exhale."

By simply controlling the breath (something called conscious breathing or pranayama in Yoga) the panic attack was stopped. The anxiety and hyperventilation quickly subsided. Why? Because conscious breathing controls the mood. It calms the body down and stops the anxiety. Conversely, an anxious mood gives rise to an anxious breath: hyperventilation.

The triage nurse was actually doing two powerful things at once. She (or he) was teaching the patient how to breathe on purpose instead of on autopilot. She was also touching the patient with her healing hands. The patient's episode of panic attack would often be "cured" by the time I saw the patient. All that was left for me to do was to rule out heart attack and other causes of hyperventilation, like pulmonary embolism (blood clot) or diabetic ketoacidosis, administer a big dose of reassurance, then refer the patient for further treatment.

Most often, patients would press for a Xanax prescription. A quick fix that treats a symptom is what most patients in America have been conditioned to demand. Fixing the problem at its root can be much more complicated and time consuming.

Many times, the panic attack was a direct result of *running out* of Valium (diazepam) or Xanax (alprazolam). According to Harris Stratyner, of The National Council on Alcoholism and Drug Dependence, "Dependence on benzodiazepines like Xanax is a serious problem, especially among young women. Frequently, it's not because they've been abusing the drugs; it can be caused by following the prescription their doctor gave them."

During my ER years, I often wished I had a treatment to offer other than what mainstream medicine was serving up. I realized I was treating patients whose bodies and minds had already succumbed to the mountain of stress they were under in their day-to-day lives: job stress, financial stress, relationship stress, etc. The medical world seemed to provide little or no emphasis on prevention. Just treat the symptoms with a quick fix and move on. Working in a busy trauma center, there was little or no time to counsel patients on lifestyle changes that would keep them from a return ER visit. I often thought that if patients had an effective way to deal with stress, many 911 calls could be avoided. Years later, after studying

Eastern Medicine, I would discover two of the most important keys to feeling calm and balanced: Breath Meditation (pranayama) and Mantra Meditation.

General Anxiety Disorder

In contrast to panic attack, patients with *chronic* stress and anxiety are often given a diagnosis of General Anxiety Disorder, or GAD. They suffer from a persistent, excessive and unrealistic worry about everyday things that lasts for six months or more.

GAD patients are overly concerned about money, health, work or relationship problems. The degree of worry is out of proportion to the real circumstances. Sometimes just the thought of getting through the day produces anxiety. They don't know how to stop the worry cycle and feel it is beyond their control. Many even realize that their anxiety is more intense than the situation warrants.

GAD affects 6.8 million adults, or about 3 percent of the U.S. population, in any given year. Women are twice as likely to be affected.

When the anxiety level is mild, people with GAD can function socially and be gainfully employed.

Anxiety and Its Message

Why have anxiety and panic attack become so prevalent in modern society? Is there a message here?

It is no wonder that anxiety is found everywhere. Anxiety has become embedded in our culture -- the anxiety to be loved, to be happy, to have money, to keep up with the neighbors, to *be* somebody.

Our very way of life breeds it, from the 24-hour news to the stress at work to problems at home. Anxiety has become the inevitable effect of the way we live. This epidemic of unrest (and attention deficit disorder, or ADD) is fueled by the "modern lifestyle," a lifestyle of consumerism and overstimulation that fails to nourish the Soul.

The restless Soul desperately wants to find peace and contentment, freedom from anxiety. However, anxiety cannot be removed until its cause is addressed. Dr. David Frawley, author of *Mantra Yoga and Primal Sound*, had this to say: "If your reality is based on the superficial, on consumerism and pettiness, anxiety will always be part of your life."

However, if your reality becomes based on perception of truth through meditation, self-inquiry and self-realization, you can rid yourself of anxiety. Self-inquiry means asking yourself questions, like "Who am I?" and "What am I doing here." It is a first step toward revealing the causes of stress and anxiety and discovering your place in the world.

Self-realization means becoming aware of your purpose and place in the Universe, that you are a Being of Light made of conscious energy. You are made of the same stuff as the Ultimate Reality, or Source, just like a drop of ocean water is not different from its source, the ocean.

What Really Causes Depression and Anxiety?

Most people feel depressed at times. Life often presents us with challenging situations

-- a death in the family, a divorce, the loss of a job. It is normal to feel sad, lonely, scared or nervous in such situations.

For some people, however, the sad or the anxious feeling will not go away, even long after a traumatic event has passed. Everyday functioning becomes increasingly difficult. Nearly half of those diagnosed with depression are also diagnosed with anxiety disorder. Fortunately, both conditions are treatable.

Depression is a condition in which a person feels sad, discouraged, unmotivated -- disinterested in life. Seeking help is recommended if the condition lasts for more than a few weeks, especially if it includes suicidal ideation. If the episode interferes with eating, sleeping, work, school or family obligations, it is likely a "major depressive episode."

According to the World Health Organization, "Depression is a complex disorder which can manifest itself under a variety of circumstances." It can be due to a number of factors: Physical (e.g. hypothyroidism), sociological (stress-induced) and psychological (mental). Research during the last 50 years indicates that there is no *single* factor that can explain the cause for depression.

Physical Causes of Depression

If you feel anxious or depressed for more than a few weeks, make sure you first get a thorough medical workup, including comprehensive blood work that includes a detailed look at your thyroid. Depression may be caused by hypothyroidism, pancreatic cancer, brain trauma, toxins, obesity, diabetes, sleep apnea and more. In men, low testosterone is a major contributor to depression.

It is estimated that 30 to 40 percent of all patients with depression have underlying medical causes. Without a thorough workup, it is impossible to know what is causing the depression.

Mental Depression

Once physical disease is ruled out, it is time to consider the root cause of most mental depression: a lack of love and connection in life (not a lack of serotonin).

According to Ayurveda, such isolation causes pain, leaving us with feelings of wanting and lack. Life can feel dry, hardly worth living. Feelings of loneliness, anxiety, anger, depression and even suicide come to the surface.

Holistic psychology strives to lead the patient back to feelings of love and connection by reinforcing positive thoughts and emotions like gratitude, joy and contentment.

Suicide

Both depression and anxiety can carry a high risk of suicide. More people die from suicide than from automobile collisions, with the CDC reporting over 40,000 suicides in 2013. Sadly, suicide has become the number one cause of death in the U.S. military.

Most suicides are preventable according to the American Foundation for Suicide Prevention. Many patients don't receive treatment due to lack of money, social stigma or lack of knowledge about their illness.

If you are feeling suicidal, depressed and alone, help is available. *Call someone today.* Call The National Suicide Prevention Lifeline, 1-800-273-TALK, to speak with a skilled counselor, or contact the American Foundation for Suicide Prevention at afsp. org, or call 911.

It may be useful to think of psychic pain and anxiety as friends who expose the errors of our ways and encourage us to make changes. We feel anxious because our lives are out of harmony with reality and with Nature. The good news is that, for many, both anxiety and depression can be effectively treated with the alternative methods covered in this book.

Yoga and Ayurveda: The Path Back To Wellness

From an Ayurvedic perspective, we are at our core healthy, whole, and happy by nature. It is important, then, to engage in habits and practices like Yoga, Tai Chi or Chi Gong that bring balance to mind, body, and Spirit. They help us to flow in harmony with nature and the natural cycles of life.

How are Ayurveda and Yoga related?

According to Dr. Frawley, "Ayurveda is the healing branch of yogic science, while Yoga (union with the Divine) is the spiritual aspect of Ayurveda."

It's important to remember that Yoga is much more than stretching. The yoga system has eight parts and the asanas (yoga poses) as seen on TV, are just one part. The last three parts, dharana (concentration), dhyana (meditation) and samadhi (absorption into bliss) have to do with meditation. That is where mantric chanting comes in -- as a form of mindful meditation that naturally leads us into a place of happiness and peace, a meditative state.

Mantra Yoga, yoga for the mind, is one of the most important parts of Ayurvedic medicine. The original definition of Yoga by the sage Patanjali is "that which calms the thought waves of the mind," thought waves being the worries and the hurries. Both Yoga for the body and yoga for the mind can be done by almost anyone, even those confined to wheelchairs (see Peggy Cappy's *Yoga For the Rest of Us* series on PBS). Yoga for the body can be as simple as gently rotating the neck or opening and closing the fists, movements that maintain a full range of motion and lubricate the joints. Yoga for the mind, Mantra Yoga can be as simple as chanting *OM* (*AUM*).

Pratyahara: Management of the Sensory Input

Another yogic practice important to mental and spiritual health is pratyahara, the fifth and least understood limb of yoga. Pratyhara is best defined as "management of the sensory input" or "turning down the noise." A good example of pratyahara would be turning off the TV or radio, the Nintendo or Facebook, then cloud watching, hiking in the woods, sitting by a creek, or saying a mantra instead.

Video games and fast paced media (Facebook and Twitter) are the opposite of meditation and examples of poor pratyahara. They scatter the mind and encourage it to cultivate patterns of ADD. Each episode of the nightly news, with its "if it bleeds, it leads" mindset, is truly disturbing to the psyche.

What Can You Do?

"Don't put junk food in your body and don't put junk food (media overstimulation) into the mind" is one of the credos of Ayurveda.

Avoid watching programs and TV commercials that assault you with a rapid succession of images that change every two or three seconds or less. A short attention span can make all perceptions and relationships shallow and unsatisfying. Spend more time outdoors enjoying Nature.

Tips For Better Pratyahara:

Limit your TV watching to programs you really want to see.
Do not watch TV at random.
Use the mute button during commercials.
Avoid violence and horror.

—

My teacher used to say, "The switch is always on," meaning that impressions, good and bad, are always going into the psyche. These impressions, called samskaras in yoga, remain in the subconscious. Negative and violent impressions can lie in the psyche like a rusting bicycle at the bottom of a well, muddying the waters of our lives.

The Holistic Psychologist

The holistic psychologist relies on therapies that are mainstream in India, yet still considered alternative in the West. Three of the main tools used by the Ayurvedic Psychological Counselor (APC) are:

1. Mantra Meditation
2. Pranayama (Breath Meditation)
3. Self-Inquiry (Who am I? What is my life's purpose?)

These techniques, which are common to both Yoga and Ayurveda, can be amazingly effective in calming the mind and enlightening the intellect. Self-inquiry, questioning everything, is important because many patients suffer from false beliefs that are a set up for depression. These false assumptions may include:

1. My value as a person depends on what others think of me.
2. To be happy, I must be accepted by all people at all times.
3. If someone disagrees with me, it means he doesn't like me.
4. If I make a mistake, it means I am no good.
5. In order to be happy, I must be successful in whatever I undertake.

The Ayurvedic Counselor helps clients blast through these myths by using the power of self-inquiry, Breath Meditation, and Mantra Meditation. If you prefer a holistic approach, have an open mind and want to reduce your dependency on synthetic pharmaceuticals, Ayurvedic Psychological Counseling may be right for you.

Summary

In this chapter, we explored the real causes of anxiety and depression. We learned how

Ayurveda and Yoga are related, and how Ayurveda's holistic psychology can be used to treat the maladies of the mind. We discovered how the Ayurvedic Psychological Counselor treats anxiety and stress, with tools like Mantra Meditation, Breath Meditation and Self-Inquiry.

The ultimate goal of Ayurvedic psychology is a higher awareness, a higher consciousness that can heal the mind where the trouble starts -- mental unrest on the subconscious and unconscious levels. In the next chapter we will discover how meditation, especially Mantra Meditation, is the key.

Chapter 3
Mantra Meditation

"Harnessing the power of the mind can be more effective than the drugs you have been programmed to believe you need."
                                    Bruce Lipton, Ph.D.

This chapter will answer the following questions and more:

1. What is Meditation?
2. What is Mantra?
3. What is the easiest way to meditate?

What is Meditation?

According to Sarah McLean, former education director for Deepak Chopra, and founder of the McLean Meditation Institute in Sedona, Arizona, meditation is simply the process of giving your full attention, your concentration, to whatever object you have chosen. That object could be something you can see, like a cloud or a candle flame, or something you can hear, like the sound of the ocean, or something you can do, like walking, breathing or Yoga.

Patanjali, author of *The Yoga Sutras* (Verses), described meditation as the "progressive quieting of the mind, until it reaches its source in pure silence." In the East and West, thousands practice moving meditations like Yoga, Tai Chi and Chi Gong. Others prefer a Zen-style mediation -- simply sitting, watching the thoughts come and go.

For many, a moving meditation, like Yoga, is the best place to start, especially if you have trouble sitting still. Seated meditation, like Tibetan zazen, is, for many, more suited for advanced practice.

The opposite of meditation is distraction. Unfortunately, we live in the age of distraction, the age of multitasking: texting, web surfing, email, Facebook, Twitter, 24-hour news, shopping at the mall and so on. Another major source of distraction comes from worry -- worrying about the future, regretting the past, putting ourselves down or blaming others.

Constant distraction makes us feel stressed and uncentered, overwhelmed and ungrounded. It is a massive energy drain. Learning how to focus, how to get away from distraction and concentrate again, has become one of the greatest challenges of our time.

What is the antidote for distraction? Meditation, starting with the Mantra Meditations in this book.

Why Meditate?

Meditation is Ayurveda's main tool for healing the mind. Regular meditation can help us feel less anxious and more rested. It lowers the blood pressure and boosts the immune system. Cortisol, that damaging stress hormone, goes down. In general, health is improved.

Meditation takes us out of our thinking mind and puts us into a happier place, a place of peacefulness and calm, a place where we can watch thoughts come and go like clouds in the sky. How do we get there? Where do we start? In her book, *Simple Easy Every Day Meditation*, Sarah McLean wrote, "Every meditation begins with mindfulness," bringing your attention fully into the present moment. For example, mindful eating means giving your full attention to every bite of food -- its texture, smell and taste. Is it spicy or bland? Hot or cold? Sour or sweet? Mindful breathing can be as easy as counting to two: mentally repeating "One" with every in breath and "Two" with every out breath, or "I am breathing in peacefulness and breathing out calm."

Meditation, whether on a candle flame, a breath technique or a mantra, requires only three things: your willingness to do it, your full attention and something to focus on. The ultimate purpose of meditation is to help us cultivate a state of higher awareness where we are filled with feelings of clarity and joy. For many, the most direct way to get there is Mantra Meditation.

Sanskrit Mantra: The Easiest Way to Meditate

Of all the different types of meditation, chanting Sanskrit mantras is the easiest way to meditate. No experience is necessary and side effects may include peacefulness and calm.

The general meaning of mantra is a word or phrase repeated over and over, mentally or out loud. However, Sanskrit mantras are something special. Sanskrit is the mystical language of ancient India that is also the language of mantra. Unlike other languages, Sanskrit is based on the science of sound vibration. Word meanings are secondary. The most important thing is the effect of the sound vibration itself on the body and the mind.

The best example of a Sanskrit mantra is *AUM* (*OM*). The sound vibrations produced by chanting *AUM* create feelings of peacefulness and harmony in *all the cells* of the body. Over time, *AUM* chanting leads to happiness and health, contentment and oneness. These good feelings, these positive emotions, are the goal of Ayurvedic Psychology.

AUM (OM): The Core Mantra Meditation

For beginners, I recommend a mantra practice that starts with *AUM*. *AUM* is the most important mantra and the source of all other mantras. If you want to learn just one mantra, make it *AUM*. Other mantras can be added to your family of mantras as you go along.

The three letters of A-U-M represent the three levels of consciousness: waking, dreaming and deep sleep. By meditating on *AUM* we can access the fourth state of consciousness, *turiya* -- the state of unbroken awareness, or *samadhi*. A-U-M also symbolizes the beginning of the Universe, the middle and the end.

Chanting AUM stimulates the sixth chakra, the third eye, the eye of intuition. It is the best way to access the psychic realm, where clairvoyance and telepathy become every day occurrences.

AUM is an antidote for anxiety and depression. Just twenty minutes of *AUM* chanting twice a day, combined with conscious breathing, can be enough to hit the reset button, taking the mind from restless and agitated to peaceful and calm. While in California I met one group of yogis whose sole (Soul) meditation practice was chanting *AUM*.

Thousands of years ago, there were no corner drug stores, no prescription pads. The sages of old, in deepest meditation (samadhi), perceived a better way to calm the mind -- by chanting mantras from this Yoga of Sound tradition. It is the yoga of music and mantra, of *AUM* chanting and more.

How Do Mantras Work?

"If you want to find the secrets of the Universe, think in terms of energy, frequency and vibration."

Nikola Tesla

All mantras work on the basis of sound waves (energy vibrations) and thought waves (intentions). The physical body and the energy (astral) body are extremely sensitive to sound. Some sounds, like the ocean surf, or a harp playing or *AUM* chanting, are soothing to the nervous system. Other sounds, like fingernails on a chalkboard or the cacophony of a jack hammer, make the body cringe.

Sanskrit mantras, like *AUM*, are sound formulas, rooted in yogic science, that have profound effects on the body-mind. Just as a chemical formula, like aspirin, has an effect on the body (i.e., anti-platelet and anti-inflammatory), a sound formula, like *AUM*, has its own effect on the body-mind, inducing peacefulness and harmony.

Both music and mantra use the power of sound waves to elevate the mood without antidepressants. Music, like mantra, goes directly into the part of the brain that has to do with mood and emotions. Consider the transporting music of Celine Dion, Josh Groban or Louis Armstrong. The mind's focus changes in an instant, after just a few notes. Troubles disappear. Such is the power of music.

While Western music can be therapeutic, Sanskrit mantras and Indian ragas (intricate musical scales that mirror the human emotions) go much further in the sound healing process. Their vibrations have the power to heal at the subconscious and unconscious levels, where the roots of much psychological unrest are found.

Healing mantras don't force the mind to be quiet. When repeated long enough, these mantras allow the mind to experience the silence already there. Calming the noisy mind allows you to enter into a deeper level of awareness, a place of peacefulness and calm. Mantric sound waves change the energetic structure of the mind and dissolve the problem (the worry) on a subconscious level, whereas thinking about the problem can reinforce it.

Mantra is especially good for those with ADD, a condition called *rajas* (hyperactivity) in Ayurveda. Ideally suited for those who can't sit still, Mantra Meditation can even be done walking.

Thanks to Ayurveda's methods for treating the mind, it is possible to get away from the old paradigm of "see doctor, get prescription, take pill."

The Elephant and the Mind

Along with healing sound waves, mantra meditation works on another level: mantras give the restless mind something to hold onto.

A great example comes to us in a story from Mahatma Gandhi's childhood.

As a boy, Gandhi had a wise teacher, a family servant named Rhamba. She would remind him that the practice of mantra is much like the training of an elephant. The young elephant is naturally restless, scattered and undisciplined. Untrained, he wanders through the fruit market with a restless trunk, creating chaos. Merchants scatter as tables overturn and mangoes and bananas tumble to the ground.

The wise elephant trainer will give that young elephant a stick of bamboo to hold with his trunk. Doing so calms the animal down by giving him something to hold onto. All settled, he strides through the market like a sage, with a new calmness and serenity.

The untrained mind is just like that untrained elephant -- undisciplined and easily distracted. It needs something to hold on to. If your mind is holding on to a worry, a grievance, a resentment, or a bad memory, give it a stick of bamboo. Give it a mantra.

Over time, Sanskrit mantra can gather and focus the mind's energy like a laser beam, and lead from concentration (*dharana*) to meditation (*dhyana*) to *samadhi* (deepest meditation, or "absorption"). Mantra Meditation is the fastest way to *samadhi*, though the journey may take some time.

Mantra helps us achieve the original aim of yoga: "calming the thought waves of the mind." Mantric chanting is the doorway to the meditative state, a state of peacefulness and contentment.

TM: A Mantra Meditation Twice a Day

There are a lot of misconceptions about mantra, many of which come from the public's perception of TM, or Transcendental Meditation. The TM movement was famously started in 1969 by Maharishi Mahesh Yogi, who became guru to the Beatles for a brief period of time.

TM is a simple form of Mantra Meditation, 20 minutes, twice a day. TM recommends short *bija* (seed) mantras, like *Shrim* and *Sham*, prescribed based on one's age and gender. These bija mantras have no literal meaning. Rather, they bathe the body-mind with a healing sound vibration, like a celestial harp. They tune the mind to a different vibration.

Many famous people, like David Lynch, Jerry Seinfeld and Ellen Degeneres are proponents of TM. Jerry has been practicing TM mantra meditation for decades. Ellen has said that mantra meditation was the *only* form of meditation that could calm down her mind.

At the Chopra Center in Southern California, anxiety patients are encouraged to take a course called "Primordial Sound Healing," which is in many ways similar to TM. (Dr. Chopra was formerly Medical Director for the Maharishi Mahesh Ayurvedic Health Center.) Patients are given a short Sanskrit mantra to chant twice daily.

Unfortunately, both TM and Primordial Sound Healing can be expensive for many. According to the TM website, the price of TM training in 2015 is $960, marked down from $1,500. For that sum one is given a "secret" mantra, instructions and "lifetime support."

In contrast, the most important Ayurvedic/ Yoga of Sound mantras are no longer secret and can be found in books like this one. This comprehensive family of mantras includes *Vedic* mantras like the *Triambakam*, for power and protection, *Tantric* mantras for creating and moving energy, and *Bhakti* (devotional) mantras to open the heart to love. Each of these three branches is addressed in my book, *The Mystical Chakra Mantras*, with links to YouTube for proper pronunciation.

Mantra Meditation is for everyone with a heart and mind open to alternative medicine. It is for everyone who wants to connect with Spirit.

The Yoga of Sound

While TM mantras and Primordial Sound Healing can effectively calm the mind, they make up only a small portion of the thousands of mantras in the Yoga of Sound (YOS) tradition. The YOS is a complete treasure-trove of mantras, not only for calming the mind, but also for helping us accomplish all four goals

—

of life: *Artha, Kama, Dharma* and *Moksha*...
Wealth, Love, Life's Purpose and Immortality.

Artha refers to the goal of material abundance,
wealth in all of its forms, including money,
success, fame and fortune. In Ayurvedic
thought, it's OK to make a lot of money, as
long as it is used for good purposes. A classic
Artha mantra is *OM Shrim Maha Lakshmiyei
Swaha.*

The second goal is *Kama*, which refers to
pleasure in all its forms, including divine
love, romantic love and sensual pleasure.
Our bodies are wired for pleasure. However,
like all of life's gifts, it should be enjoyed in
moderation. If pleasure becomes an addiction,
it can lead to exhaustion.

A powerful *Kama* mantra for a woman to
attract a man is the Soulmate Mantra:

*Sat Pa-tim De-hi Para-mesh-va-ra
Swa-ha*

"Give to me a man of truth, with perfect
masculine attributes, who will honor my
goddess nature."

For proper pronunciation of this mantra, please see my YouTube titled "Mantra for a Woman to Attract a Soulmate."

To be effective, *Artha* and *Kama* mantras should be repeated at least 108 times a day. This more formal mantra practice requires *mala* beads (similar to rosary beads) to keep track of repetitions.

The third goal of life is *Dharma*, which refers to one's life purpose, or duty. *Dharma* should include compassionate service. An example of a *Dharma* mantra is *Lokah Samastha Sukhino Bhavantu*, or "May all beings be happy and free."

The fourth goal is *Moksha*, which refers to immortality, enlightenment and liberation from the conditioned mind. One of the best *Moksha* mantras is the *Gayatri*, a meditation on the Light of spiritual consciousness, covered in detail in Chapter 4.

Mantra and *Pranayama*

Yoga Tip: Mantra necessarily involves pranayama, or conscious breathing, the fourth limb of yoga and yet another way to calm the mind.

One thing that goes hand in hand with chanting is breathing. The best way to breathe is conscious breathing, to breathe with a purpose. Normally our breath is on autopilot; it's shallow and we don't give it much thought. I call it barely breathing. It barely gives us the energy and oxygen we really need. Breathing is free, so why take in just a little air when you can take in a lot?

So how could we breathe to calm the nervous system and, at the same time, energize the body?

The most basic *pranayama* is the Yogic Breath, a type of long deep breathing that uses the lung's full capacity. The Yogic Breath is the fastest way to calm the mind and nervous system, while increasing energy and oxygenation. Think of it as a yogic antidote for anxiety and hyperventilation.

Benefits of Mantra Meditation and Chanting

Sanskrit mantras are nothing less than mystical sound formulas, each one a small package of sound wave energy that has a specific effect on the body-mind.

Here are just a few of the benefits of Mantra Meditation:

1. Relief of emotional pain, like anger, sadness, disappointments, resentments and low self-esteem

2. Cultivation of *sattva* -- feelings of centeredness, relaxation and calm

3. A decrease in insomnia, anxiety and depression

An increase in inspiration and creativity

5. An increase in feelings of connection with others and with Spirit

An eminent British physician, Dr. Alan Watkins, found that chanting can lower

—

both heart rate and blood pressure. Even listening to mantric chants normalizes adrenalin levels and brain wave patterns. He found that chanting in a group promotes a sense of well-being and helps us bond with those around us, something Native peoples everywhere have known for millennia.

Dr. Alfred Tomatis of the French Academy of Science and Medicine found that chanting aids in getting over addictions like smoking, alcohol and drugs. It helps us control our mind and emotions and eliminate negative thoughts.

Researchers at Cleveland University found that the rhythmic tones involved in chanting create a harmonious effect in the body called the Neuro-linguistic effect, or NLE. The vibration of the sound calms the nervous system and induces a cascade of the naturally healing chemicals. A profound sense of peace is produced. The research concluded that chanting can soothe all our bodily systems and activate the body's natural healing process.

Healing the Spirit

Unlike Western psychiatry, Mantra Meditation goes beyond the body-mind to the realm of Spirit. Mantric chanting supports spirituality, regardless of one's religion.

For thousands of years cultures around the world have used chanting to connect with the Divine, from Sanskrit chanting in India and Tibet, to the chanting of Native Peoples in North and South America, to the Gregorian chants in Europe, to the chanting of Amen (AUMen) in churches around the world.

By focusing our energies on higher spiritual thoughts, chanting can bring about a transformation that leads us closer to the Divine, closer to Oneness. Many psychologists believe that chanting mantras, especially the names of the Divine, helps us become aware of, and even unite with the Ultimate Reality.

Summary

There are many beneficial effects to mantric chanting, both physical and psychological. As a medical doctor, I used to prescribe pills for both anxiety and depression. As an Ayurvedic mantra practitioner, I now prescribe healing Sanskrit mantras.

"Harnessing the power of the mind can be more effective than the drugs you have been programmed to believe you need."
                                   Bruce Lipton, Ph.D.

Here is a table outlining some of the risks and benefits of Pill Therapy versus Mantra Therapy:

Pill Therapy	**Mantra Therapy**
Prescription needed from MD	Self-healing by patient at home
Adverse side effects common	Beneficial side effects common
Addictions common	Not addictive
Withdrawal symptoms possible	No withdrawal symptoms

My hope is that one day Mantra Meditation will become the new psychiatry, a path back to wellness and happiness without prescription drugs and their side effects.

"Mantras are important medicines in themselves, and have been lauded as such since Vedic times
Dr. David Frawley

Mantra Q & A

How do I get started with Mantra Meditation?

Start with *AUM* chanting.

First create a quiet sacred space.
Next state your intention: "I intend to feel peaceful, calm and connected."

Then chant *AUM* for seven minutes twice a day, using my YouTube, *The Cosmic AUM* as a guide. As you become more comfortable with chanting, add the rest of the Seven Essential Mantras from Chapter 4 to your family of mantras (see YouTube playlist at end of book).

—

Do I have to chant the mantras, or will I benefit from just listening?

You will benefit either way. Start by listening. Join in when you feel ready. Experiment with chanting the mantras out loud, then whispered, then silently to yourself.

Should I throw away my Xanax?

No. Medications for anxiety like Xanax need to be tapered slowly to reduce withdrawal symptoms, under the close supervision of the prescribing physician.

Chapter 4
Seven Essential Mantras

In this chapter I will share with you seven of the most important healing mantras from the Ayurvedic/Yoga of Sound tradition:

AUM (OM)
OM Shanti Shanti Shan-ti-hi
Asato Ma Satgamaya
Lokah Samastha
Sat Nam
The Gayatri
The Triambakam (Mahamrityunjaya)

Each of these mantras is soothing to the nervous system and calming to the body. Each promotes oneness and connection with Spirit.

Sanskrit mantras are like apps on a smart phone.
Need an app to soothe anxiety?
Chant *OM Shanti Shanti Shanti-hi*

—

Need an app to help overcome the stuck energy of depression?
Chant *Sat Nam*.

Need an app for enlightenment?
Chant the *Gayatri* mantra.

Of course, proper pronunciation, along with frequent repetition, is essential for achieving the desired results. Each of these mantras is readily available on YouTube and iTunes (see YouTube playlist at end of book).

AUM: The Cosmic Sound

Why do we chant AUM?

We chant *AUM* for harmony and oneness, for peacefulness and calm, for happiness and health. Chanting *AUM* not only harmonizes the mind, its sound vibrations harmonize every cell in the physical body.

What is the best way to chant AUM?
AUM comes in two forms. The long form, A-U-M, is used when *AUM* is chanted by itself. One big breath = one long *AUM*.

The short form (*OM*) is often used as a prefix for other mantras, like *OM Shanti, Shanti, Shanti-hi.*

The long *AUM* is like a three-syllable word -- there's the Ahh, the Uuu and the Mmm.

Open wide and say Ahh to begin.
End with lips together, creating a firm Mmm sound.

The Uuu will naturally happen in between: AAAUUUMMM.

Be sure to save the final third of your *AUM* chant for the Mmm sound. The consonant "M" creates the energy of groundedness and stability.

OM Shanti Shanti Shan-ti-hi

This peace mantra is often chanted in yoga studios as a beautiful way to close out the class. Think of it as a mantric antidote to stress.

Shanti means peace -- a dynamic peace: peace of mind, body and Spirit. However, the soothing effect of chanting *OM Shanti* goes beyond any meaning or definition of the words.

When the body is bathed in the sound waves of *OM Shanti*, a *feeling* of peacefulness is both created and *experienced*. The sound of *Shaaan* -- the sound *waves* produced by chanting *Shaaan* -- are soothing to the nervous system and relaxing to the body. It's like giving ourselves a sound bath, a gong bath, a mantra bath.

Chanting *OM Peace Peace Peace* simply does not have the same effect. If you are having a tough day, and need a big dose of peacefulness, find a quiet space, take three long deep breaths and chant this mantra 27-108 times. You will feel better.

I have a good friend in the Virgin Islands who has used this mantra successfully for years. Whenever a "relationship issue" crops up, he goes into an adjacent room and chants *OM Shanti Shanti Shanti-hi*, until peacefulness returns.

Notice that *OM* (the short form of *AUM*) is used here as a prefix -- a prefix that connects us immediately with that "higher vibration" that so many artists have sung about: the *OM* vibration, the frequency of the highest consciousness, the highest awareness. It has been called Christ consciousness, Buddha consciousness, Shiva consciousness, and so on.

Asato Ma Satgamaya

I call this next mantra the reality check mantra. It comes to us directly from the Upanishads (Brihadaranayka Upanishad 1.iii.28), among the most revered teachings from India:

A-sa-to Ma Sat Ga-ma-ya
Ta-ma-so Ma Jyo-tir Ga-ma-ya
Mrit-yor-ma Am-ri-tam Ga-ma-ya

Lead me from the unreal to the real
Lead me from the darkness to the Light
Lead me from death to immortality

Upanishadic mantras are truly Universal, and may be used with any spiritual path. The seeker who chants this mantra wants to be led from the *a-sat* (the untrue) to the *Sat*, the true. Here *Sat* refers to our true Self, our Soul-Self, the blissful consciousness that ever was, is and will be.

In line two we chant *Tamaso Ma*, lead us from the darkness of the *tamasic* state, the state of ignorance, to the place of Light (*Jyotir*), the place of knowledge.

The final line is *Mrityor Ma Amritam Gamaya*, lead me from death to the *Amrita*, the nectar, of immortality. This is not a prayer to live for endless years on heaven or earth. According to Dr. Frawley, it is a mantric prayer to the Divine for assistance in realizing the following truth:

"I was never born, nor can ever die, as I am not the body, mind and intellect. I am the eternal, blissful consciousness that underlies all creation."

If we depend too much on attachments to things that are not permanent or not real, life will be painful. Getting too attached to life's material things inevitably brings disappointment, like building a sandcastle that will always be washed back into the sea. Being beyond time and space, consciousness (awareness) itself can never be washed away by the tides of time.

As we become more and more detached from the material world, desires naturally decrease. We realize that the things of the world are impermanent and cannot bring us lasting happiness.

Lokah Samastha Sukhino Bhavantu

Lokah Samastha is the happiness mantra. Translated as "May all beings everywhere be happy and free," it has been called the ultimate yogic prayer. *All beings* includes the one who is chanting.

Here's the breakdown:

Lo-kah: a plane of existence (We live on Earth *Lokah*. Next stop: Astral (heavenly) *Lokah*)

Sa-mas-tha: all beings....all creatures everywhere

Suk-hi-no: feelings of happiness, joy and freedom

Bha-van-tu: to cultivate the feeling of, the *bhava*

Sanskrit mantras have been called energized prayers. As you chant this mantric prayer to the Ultimate Reality, think "Grant all beings, including myself, a life filled with happiness, joy and freedom."

Chanting the mantra in English is a good affirmation. However, chanting the mantra in Sanskrit goes further. It creates the feeling, the *bhava*, the experience of happiness, joy and freedom.

Sat Nam: A Kundalini Antidote For Depression

Our next mantra is *Sat Nam*, one of the simplest, yet most powerful of mantras from the Kundalini Yoga tradition. Kundalini Yoga is based on the *chakras*, the seven energy centers that lie along the spine of the energy (astral) body.

The Kundalini definition of depression is stuck energy, energy that needs to move. The sound vibration of *Sat Nam* moves the energy from the lower *chakras* to the upper *chakras*. According to master Kundalini yogi, Ravi Singh, chanting the *Sat Nam* mantra is the best antidote for the stuck energy of depression.

Sat (rhymes with dot) means truth. *Nam* (rhymes with mom) means to name, or to identify with. Taken together, *Sat Nam* can be translated "the truth within." As you chant this mantra, ask yourself, "What is my truth within?" Answers will come. Truth is perceived by silencing the mind through meditation. Then we can enter a heightened state of awareness in which we are conscious of our eternal nature.

Chanting Sat Nam has the power to clear the subconscious mind of old wounds and old programs that keep us from Self-realization, from realizing our Oneness with the Divine.

—

Chanting this mantra is most effective when combined with a *mudra*, a hand position. Use either prayer *mudra*, with palms together at the chest, or steeple *mudra*, with hands interlaced and raised high overhead, like a cosmic antenna, index fingers opposed and stretching upward together to create a steeple.

Chakra Balance

Another Kundalini Yoga treatment for depression is chakra balancing.

Chakra balance leads to groundedness, stability and good instincts -- to feelings of oneness, centeredness and connection. Chakra balance is best achieved by chanting the mystical chakra mantras, from *Lam*, the mantra for the first chakra, to *AUM*, the mantra for the sixth chakra. These chakra mantras activate (energize and balance) each of the energy centers of the subtle body, the acupuncture body.

Yoga Tip: The mantra system works on the chakra system.

It is not a coincidence that there are 50 letters in the Sanskrit alphabet and 50 key points (petals) in the *chakra* system. These "petals" are not literal flower petals. They are key points in the energy (acupuncture) body. Each letter of the Sanskrit alphabet stimulates (energizes and balances) one of the fifty "petals" of the *chakra* system, like acupuncture with sound waves instead of needles.

For more information on the *chakra* system, and the secrets of *chakra* balance, please see my book, *The Mystical Chakra Mantras*, where you can learn how to balance your own *chakras* with the Yoga of Sound.

The *Gayatri*: Queen of All Mantras

For many who meditate, one goal is enlightenment, the realization of our place in the Universe beyond time and space. One of the best mantras for enlightenment is the *Gayatri*, a meditation on the Spiritual Light.

Gayatri means "She who protects the singer." It is a mantra to help us transition from this world to the next by focusing our attention away from the physical and onto the Light of spiritual consciousness.

The mantra starts with a salutation:

OM Bhur Bhu-va-ha Swa-ha

OM to the Earth Plane (Bhu Lokah), the Heavenly (Astral) plane, and Beyond

**Tat Sa-vi-tur Va-reen-yam
Bhar-go De-vas-ya Dhi-ma-hi
Dhi-yo Yo-nah Pra-cho-dyat**

We meditate on that glorious Light of Spiritual Consciousness. May it energize and direct our awakening

Though this mantra is more complex than the previous five, it can still be mastered in a relatively short period of time. Sanskrit pronunciation is less difficult than many languages and the rewards are great. Simply listen to the mantra on YouTube as listed in the back of the book, or iTunes, then chant when you have it down.

One of my favorite YouTube versions of this mantra is chanted by Deva Premal (Goddess of Love) from Germany. Her mother sang this mantra to her during her nine months in the womb. As a result, she was born an enlightened human being, an advanced yogini.

The *Triambakam:* The Great Victory Over Death Mantra

OM Tri-am-ba-kam Ya-ja-ma-he Su-gan-dhim Push-ti-var-da-nam Ur-va Ruk-ha-mi-va Bhan-da-naan Mrit-yor Mok-shi-ya Maam-ri-tat

OM to the One Essence that permeates everything like a fragrance.

Protect me from illness during this life. Help me to pass from death to immortality as easily as the ripe fruit falls from the vine.

This is the great "Victory Over Death" mantra, the *Maha-mrit-yun-jaya.* It is widely chanted in India and Tibet for good health and protection while living and, as the end of life approaches, for transitioning from this world to the next with ease and grace. The mystical vibrations of this mantra provide physical protection and mental and spiritual comfort.

In 2002, I went on a pilgrimage to India with my Yoga of Sound mentor, Russill Paul (Anirud Jaidev), of Chennai. Our home base was Shantivanam (Forest of Peace), a Hindu-Christian ashram in Tamil Nadu, South India. To the Hindu, God is One, the One with many faces. We chanted to Jesus in the morning and Shiva at night.

One evening, my wife and I walked with Russill to a nearby funeral pyre on the sacred Kaveri River, the Ganges of the South. A body, swaddled in cotton gauze, was being cremated by the intense blaze of the fire. With the family's blessing, we chanted both the *Gayatri* mantra and the *Triambakam* to help the departing Soul with his transition.

You don't have to wait until you are dying to chant this mantra, however. It is also a mantra for power, protection and disease prevention while still living. Chanted daily, it can protect the chanter from illness and misfortune like a forcefield made of sound energy.

A swami friend of mine, Nandi, told me how this mantra saved his life. While in South India he had been rappelling down a cliff to explore some yogi caves there. Midway down the steep face, a huge swarm of angry bees descended upon him and his climbing partner. The partner was attacked, sustaining hundreds of beestings. Almost stung to death, he eventually recovered in the hospital.

On the other hand, Nandi was untouched. He had been doing a mantra sadhana (practice) for almost 40 days, chanting the *Triambakam* mantra 1,008 times a day. His body was projecting a sonic forcefield. His cells were putting out a loud vibrating "Do Not Disturb" sign.

The *Triambakam* mantra is also a Sanskrit sound formula that boosts the immune system directly by means of sound vibrations. Its effect is similar to the Mozart Effect, where listening to music fortifies the immune system by increasing blood levels of interleukin, an

—

important immune system booster, from 12-14 percent.

A Sanskrit mantra is a word which protects just by the virtue of being repeated.
                                    Pandit Tigunait

The *Triambakam* mantra is as relevant today as it was in ages past. For maximum effect, proper pronunciation of this mantra is essential. Please listen to my YouTube recording, *Mahamrityunjaya: The Great Victory Over Death Mantra*, to hear how this mantra has been chanted for thousands of years.

The mantra should be chanted a minimum of nine times a day for preventive maintenance; 108 repetitions is better. For maximum power and protection, if you have a serious illness or other threat, 1,008 times a day for 40 days is recommended.

As death approaches, I recommend playing a recording of this mantra for the one who is dying. Dying patients can hear, even if they are comatose. The sense of hearing is the last of the five senses to depart the physical body.

Tuning in to the mystical vibrations produced by chanting this mantra helps the body-mind-Spirit transition with ease and grace. It makes dying "as easy as a ripe fruit falling from the vine." Chanting this mystical mantra also helps take away the fear of death, the root of many of today's anxieties. It is a mantra that helps us address death head on.

Bonus Mantra: A Celtic Chant for Enlightenment

My favorite Celtic chant is *The Long Time Sun*, an old Irish folk song, traditionally sung at the beginning of a journey:

May the Long Time Sun Shine Upon You
All Love Surround You
And the Pure Light Within You
Guide Your Way On
Sat Nam

What is the Long Time Sun? It's the light that's always shining from within...that *namaste* Light. This chant is nothing less than a meditation on the inner Light, the Light of Spiritual Consciousness. It is a Celtic *Gayatri*.

A most soothing version of *The Long Time Sun* is readily available on YouTube and iTunes, featuring the angelic voice of Snatam Kaur. The song ends with the Sanskrit *Sat Nam*, the vibration of the truth within. This time the *Sat Nam* chant has a calming effect, with a prolonged *Saaat*, and a short *Nam*.

How to Chant: Start with 10 Minutes Twice A Day

First, create a sacred space, free of distraction. Then take three long, deep breaths, right hand over the heart.

Next set an intention: "I am happy, peaceful and content."

Finally, chant all seven mantras in sequence, nine times each, as a sound healing meditation using YouTube or iTunes as a guide. Listen at first, then join in when you're ready. It only takes about ten minutes to chant them all. The most auspicious time to chant is at sunrise and sunset -- at *sandhya*, the junction of the day and the night.

Another method is to chant any of the above healing mantras individually, 54-108 times, paying special attention to the breath (long deep breathing). Use mala (rosary) beads to keep track. First, chant the mantra out loud, preferably with the eyes closed. As time goes on, try chanting the mantras in a whisper, then silently to yourself.

I offer these mantras to you as a form of complementary medicine -- a sound healing alternative to prescription drugs for the treatment of mild to moderate anxiety and depression. Discover which mantra or mantras resonates most with you. Follow your heart and your intuition. Stick with it.

Summary

The pace of human life has accelerated to the point that each day we are saturated with more information, more over-stimulation than our ancestors met with in a lifetime. Not surprisingly, the number of people suffering from stress, anxiety, insomnia, depression and chronic health problems has skyrocketed. Many are searching for peace of mind. Peace of mind can be yours today by practicing Mantra Meditation.

All humans carry around a sound-generating device. It is the larynx, the voice box, the world's oldest musical instrument. It is always with us and can be used for communication, for music and for mantra. Five thousand years ago, in India, this sound wave generator became an important tool in Sanskrit sound healing. Just as music "tames the savage beast," Sanskrit mantra tames the restless mind.

In this book I have presented Mantra Meditation as an alternative treatment for anxiety, depression and insomnia. The mantras here offer the beginner a good place to start. With this series of chants, one can connect with the Universe with *AUM*, calm anxiety with *OM Shanti*, put on a protective cloak with the *Triambakam*, take a few steps closer to enlightenment with the *Gayatri* and say a prayer for all beings with *Lokah Samastha*.

Sanskrit mantras are a powerful force, bringing people together from around the world and creating more love on Earth.

—

For Further Study

All of the mantras in this book are readily available for listening by searching YouTube and iTunes (see YouTube playlist).

To dive deeply into the Yoga of Sound, read *The Yoga of Sound* by the amazing Russill Paul (Anirud Jaidev) and listen to his boxed set of 3 CD's: *Shabda*, *Shakti* and *Bhava* (see russillpaul.com).

For more on Ayurveda and Ayurvedic Sound Healing, see Dr. David Frawley's books, especially *Mantra Yoga and Primal Sound* and *Yoga and Ayurveda: Self-Healing and Self-Realization.*

If you are suffering from grief and loss, or anxiety and stress, I recommend *How to Put the Wag Back Into Your Tail: The Art of Releasing Painful Feelings and Taking the Journey to Joy*, by Cayenne Graves. Cayenne is a holistic Ayurvedic psychological counselor, available for phone or email consultations: wagwithjoy@gmail.com.

—

To learn more about the chakras, and how to balance your chakras with the Yoga of Sound, see *The Mystical Chakra Mantras* by Harrison Graves,

If you are new to meditation and mantra, I highly recommend Sarah McLean's books and Simple, Easy, Every Day (SEED) meditation classes, taught all over North America and Europe. Sarah, founder of the McLean Meditation Institute in Sedona, Arizona, was formerly Deepak Chopra's education director. Her workshops are both fascinating and life-changing. Her website is McLeanMeditation.com.

About The Author

Born near Athens, Ga., Dr. Graves attended the University of Georgia and the Medical College of Georgia before moving to Minneapolis for internship and residency in Emergency Medicine. His accolades include medical director, EMS, associate professor of Emergency Medicine, UNC-Chapel Hill, and election to Fellow status (FACEP) in the American College of Emergency Physicians.

An avid world traveler, Dr. G has hiked the Himalayas, done missionary work in Honduras, staffed the clinic on St. John (U.S. Virgin Islands) and sailed the high seas as a Holland America Line physician.

In 2005, Dr. Graves left the ER behind to pursue a new interest: the Yoga of Sound, aka Mantra Yoga or Ayurvedic Sound Healing. It had been his good fortune to do a year-long Yoga of Sound internship with master sound yogi, Russill Paul (Anirud Jaidev) of Chennai, author of *The Yoga of Sound*. Years in the ER taught him that many illnesses, especially those that are anxiety and stress-related,

—

can be best treated with Ayurveda, lifestyle changes and Yoga. In addition, Dr. G studied Kundalini Yoga and Ayurveda for two years at the Wisdom Fire School of Yoga in Berkeley, California.

In 2010, he began teaching Mantra Yoga, presenting Yoga of Sound workshops at yoga studios and wellness centers along the East Coast.

In 2014, he published *The Mystical Chakra Mantras: How to Balance Your Own Chakras with Mantra Yoga,* the world's first interactive eBook on mantra yoga, with links to YouTube where readers may experience the mantras.

In 2015, he began to write alternative medical blogs on hubpages.com, taught Mantra Meditation at the McLean Meditation Institute in Sedona and launched a new website, asktheHolisticMD.com. Dr. Graves currently lives in Colorado and North Carolina and is available to teach The Yoga of Sound and Mantra Meditation. Email: <u>OmNation108@ gmail.com</u>.

—

"The doctor of the future will give no medication, but will interest his patients in the care of the human frame, diet and in the cause and prevention of disease."

Thomas Edison (1903)

Bibliography

Ashley-Farrand, Thomas. *Healing Mantras,* New York: Ballantine Wellspring Books, 1999.

------------------. *Shakti Mantras* New York: Ballantine Wellspring Books, 2003.

------------------. *Chakra Mantras* San Francisco: Red Wheel/Weiser LLC, 2006.

Beck, Aaron T. *Love Is Never Enough: How Couples Can Overcome Misunderstandings, Resolve Conflicts and Solve Relationship Problems Through Cognitive Therapy.* New York: HarperCollins, 1989.

Cope, Stephen. "Gandhi and the Gita: The Making Of A Hero." *Yoga International*, Fall, 2012.

Dass, Ram. *Be Here Now*, San Cristobel, New Mexico: Lama Foundation, 1971.

Davies, James. *Cracked:The Unhappy Truth About Psychiatry*, New York, Pegasus Books, 2013.

Frawley, Dr. David. *Mantra Yoga and Primal Sound: Secrets of the Bija Mantras* Twin Lakes, Wisconsin: Lotus Press, 2010.

-----------------, *Yoga and Ayurveda: Self-Healing and Self-Realization*: Twin Lakes, Wisconsin: Lotus Press, 1999.

-----------------, *Ayurveda and the Mind*: *The Healing of Consciousness*, Twin Lakes, Wisconsin: Lotus Press, 1997.

Giri, Swami Sri Yukteswar. *The Holy Science*, Los Angeles: The Self-Realization Fellowship, 1990.

Goldsmith, J., and Moncrieff, J. "The Psychoactive Effects of Antidepressants and Their Association with Suicidality." *Currrent Drug Safety*, 6(2) (2011): 115-21.

Graves, Harrison. *The Mystical Chakra Mantras*, Asheville: OM Channel Publications, 2014.

Horwitz, Allan. *The Loss of Sadness*: *How Psychiatry Transformed Normal Sorrow into Depressive Disorder*, New York: Oxford University Press, 2007.

Khan, A., Redding,N., and Brown, W.A. "The Persistence of the Placebo Effect In Clinical Trials." *Journal of Psychiatric Research*, 42(10) (2008): 791-796.

Kirsch, Irving. *The Emperor's New Drugs: exploding the anti-depressant myth.* London: Bodly Head, 2009.

-------------- . "Challenging Received Wisdom: Anti-depressants and the Placebo Effect." *McGill Journal of Medicine.* 11(2), (2008): 219-222.

Lacasse, J.R., and Leo J. "Serotonin and Depression: A Disconnect Between the Advertisements and the Scientific Literature." *PLoS Med*, 2:. 2(12) (2005): e392.

McClean, Sarah. *Simple Easy Every Day Meditation Method,* Sedona: McClean Meditation Institute, 2013.

--------------. *Soul Centered: Transform Your LIfe in 8 Weeks With Meditation,* Carlsbad, California: Hay House, Inc., 2012.

Muktananda, Swami. *To Know The Knower,* South Fallsburg, NY: SYDA Foundation, 1979.

Paul, Russill. *The Yoga of Sound,* Novato, California: New World Library, 2004.

Rebensdorf, Alicia. "The Pimping of Prozac For PMS," http://www.alternet .org/story/11004/sarafem_%3A_the_ pimping_of_prozac_for_pms.

Saraswati, Swami Satyananda. *Kundalini Tantra,* Bihar, India: Yoga Publications Trust, 1984.

Sharfstein, S.S. "Big Pharma and American Psychiatry: The good, the bad and the ugly." *Psychiatric News,* 40 (16) (2005): 3.

Shorter, Edward. *A History of Psychiatry: From the Era of the Asylum to the Age of Prozac,* Toronto: John Wiley & Sons, 1997.

Singh, Ravi and Brett, Ana. *Kundalini Yoga* DVD, White Lion Press, 2005.

Yogananda, Paramahansa, *Autobiography of a Yogi,* United States: The Philosophical Library, 1946.

YouTube Playlist

1. The Cosmic AUM (Harrison Graves)
https://www.youtube.com/watch?v=_7dSq8bJDgM&fe

2. Lokah Samastha (Deva Premal)
https://www.youtube.com/watch?v=usJl7oiZPnc

3. The Gayatri Mantra (Deva Premal)
https://www.youtube.com/watch?v=SlUs0Wms09U&li

4. Triambakam (Mahamrityunjaya) Mantra (Harrison Graves)
https://www.youtube.com/watch?v=97efhU-U1Jc

5. Asato Ma Satgamaya (Deva Premal)
https://www.youtube.com/watch?v=l-MqTINCF_Y

6. The Long Time Sun (Snatam Kaur)
https://www.youtube.com/watch?v=T1D3ejwQiVg

---

7. The Mystical Chakra Mantras (Harrison Graves)
https://www.youtube.com/watch?v=z07Si_eWbpA

Note: See ebook version of this book for active hyperlinks.

Acknowledgements

I am filled with gratitude for all the teachers I have encountered in the past 15 years: Dr. David Frawley, leading Ayurvedic physician, author and Sanskrit scholar, Russill Paul (Anirud Jaidev), my Yoga of Sound mentor and friend, and Acharya Dharmanidhi Sarasvati, my Kundalini Yoga teacher in Berkeley.

Thank you, Sarah McLean, for inviting me to present Mantra Meditation at your amazing meditation workshops (SEED intensives) in Sedona, where you are training the teachers of tomorrow. Because of you, scores of meditation instructors are going out into the world to teach a better way to deal with anxiety and depression.

I am tremendously indebted to Rich Bard, former editor for the Miami Herald, for his sharp eye, wise suggestions and editorial advice.

Thank you, Cayenne, *mi esposa,* for 30 years of unconditional love, for your endless support and sage advice. *Muchas gracias* to

John and Chris, my two sons, for being you. You are both diamonds.

Finally, thank you to all my supporters who gave encouragement and insight as consultants and beta readers: Diane Tracy, Janet Hosmer, Maddy Epstein, Kat Giordano and Suzanne DeGross, R.N.

Disclaimer

The material in this book is for information only and not intended to be a substitute for consultation with a qualified healthcare provider. The book was written to educate and inform, to make the public more aware of Mantra Meditation from the Yoga of Sound tradition as a complementary treatment for anxiety and depression.

For patients who wish to decrease or stop your prescription medications, it is crucial that you do so gradually and under the close supervision your prescribing physician. Sudden withdrawal can be dangerous, even life-threatening.

Hari OM Tat Sat.

Made in the USA
San Bernardino, CA
12 September 2017